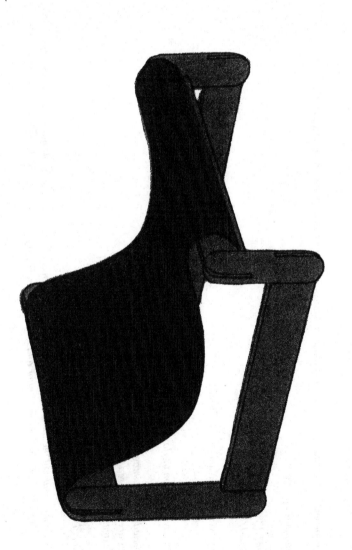

CHAIR DESIGNS

authorHOUSE®

PAULO ZAVALA Architectural and Interior Design
Phone: Email:

design by	drawn by	date	scale	job number

AuthorHouse™
1663 Liberty Drive
Bloomington, IN 47403
www.authorhouse.com
Phone: 1 (800) 839-8640

Published by AuthorHouse 12/04/2017

ISBN: 978-1-5462-1783-1 (sc)
ISBN: 978-1-5462-1782-4 (e)

Library of Congress Control Number: 2017918284

Print information available on the last page.

INTRODUCTION

I have been designing and fabricating furniture for long time. Now I want to share with you some of my Chair Designs that I think are suitable for today's way of life.

My Chairs meet the requirements of aesthetic, ergonomic and production standards actually in use and require common materials as wood, steel, reinforced concrete, leather and canvas to complete the whole project.

Fabricating the chairs myself, allowed me to understand the intricate interaction between Design and Fabrication and the final product is a mix of both elements.

I have designed these chairs under the influence of the principles of the Bauhaus Movement. Designing a Chair has been an obsession to every Architect, also me, since the very beginning of civilization.

PAULO ZAVALA Architectural and Interior Design
Phone: Email:

design by	drawn by	date	scale	job number

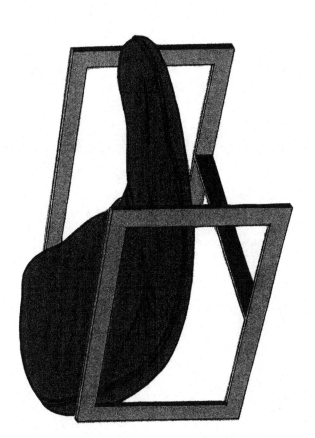

PAULO ZAVALA Architectural and Interior Design
Phone:
Email:

design by	drawn by	date	scale	job number

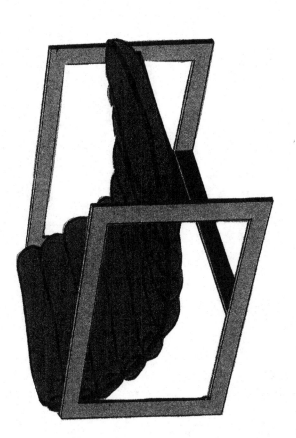

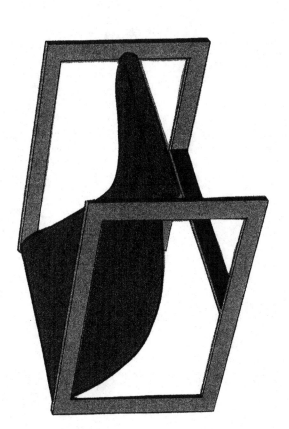

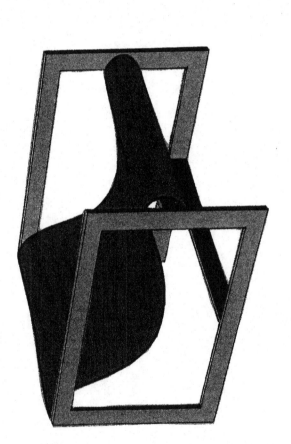

7

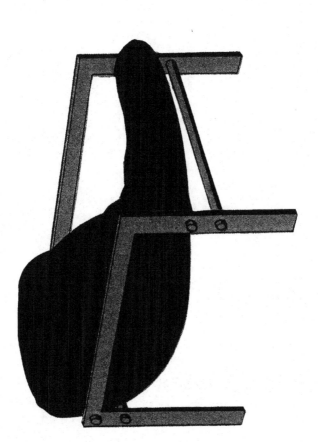

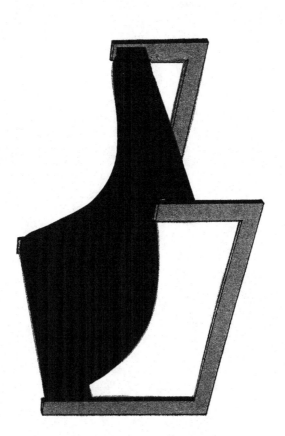

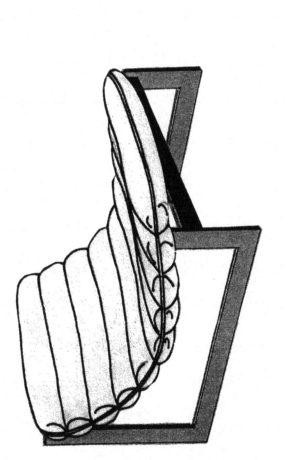

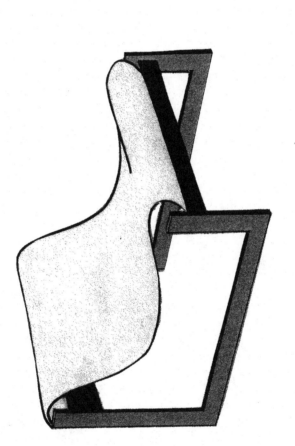

15

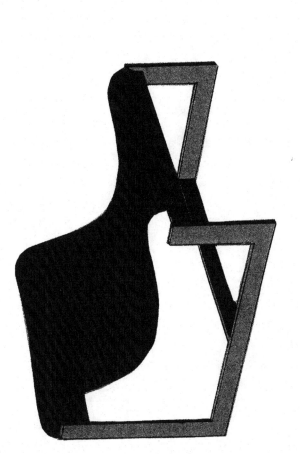

PAULO ZAVALA Architectural and Interior Design
Phone:
Email:

design by	drawn by	date	scale	job number

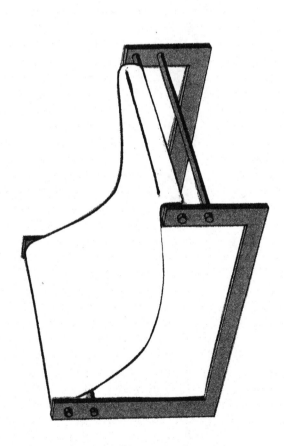

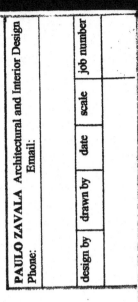

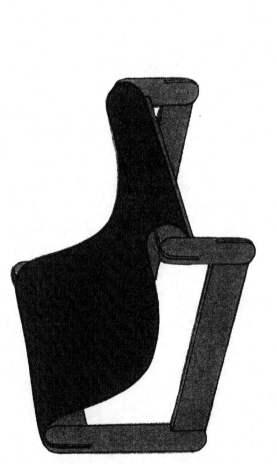

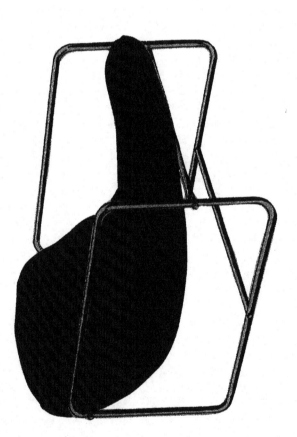

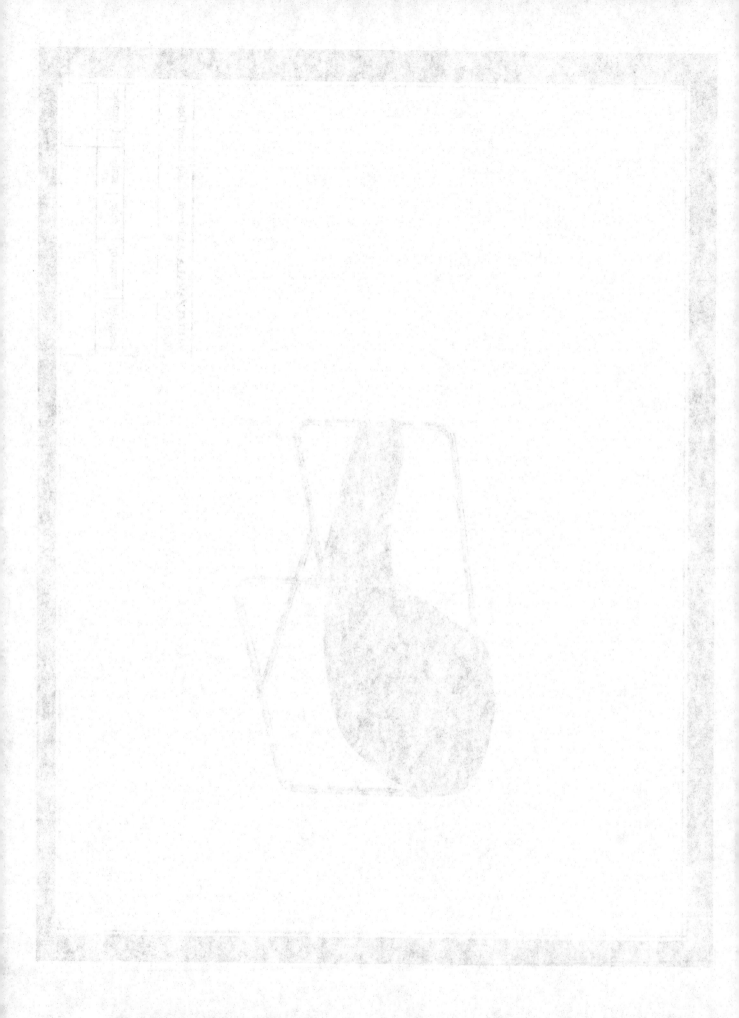

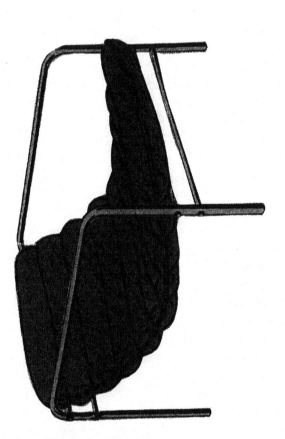

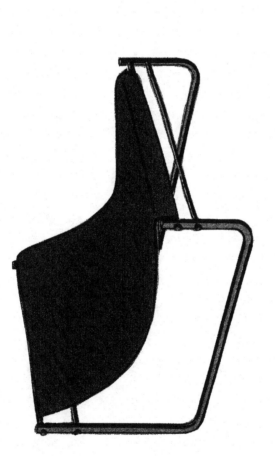

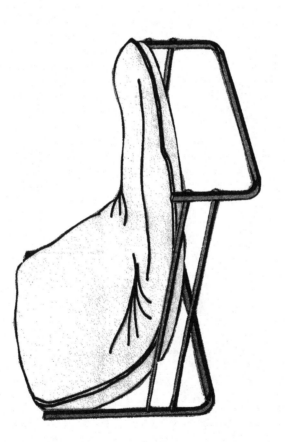

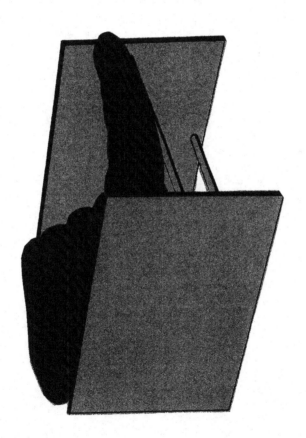

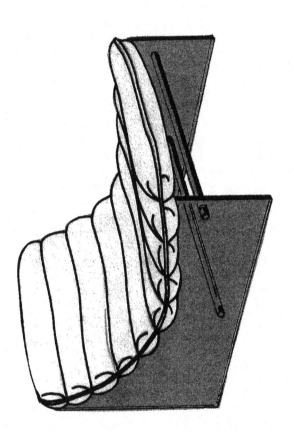

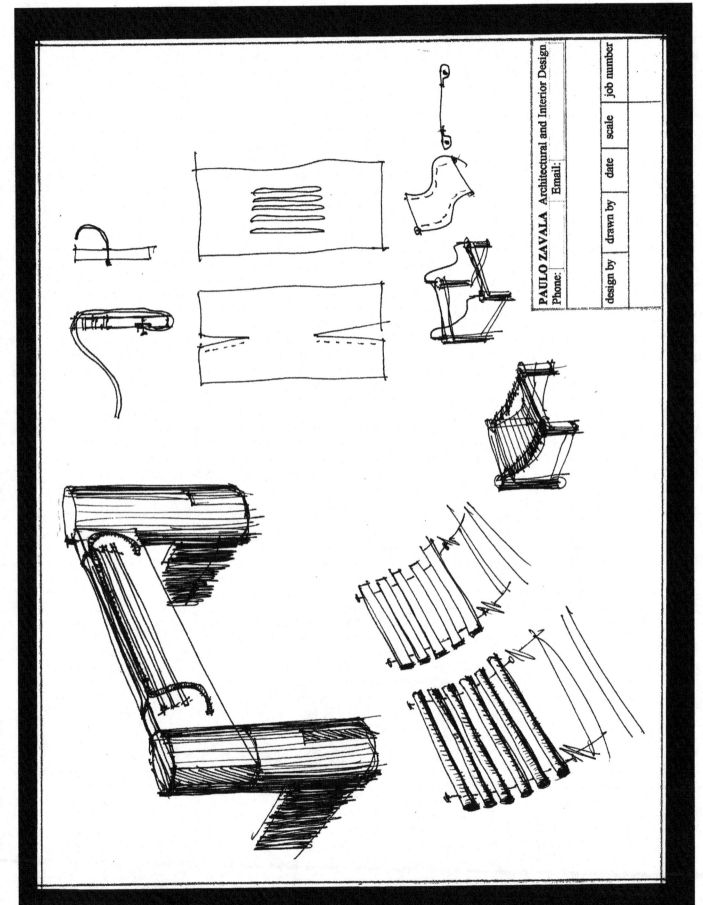

PAULO ZAVALA Architectural and Interior Design
Phone: Email:

design by	drawn by	date	scale	job number

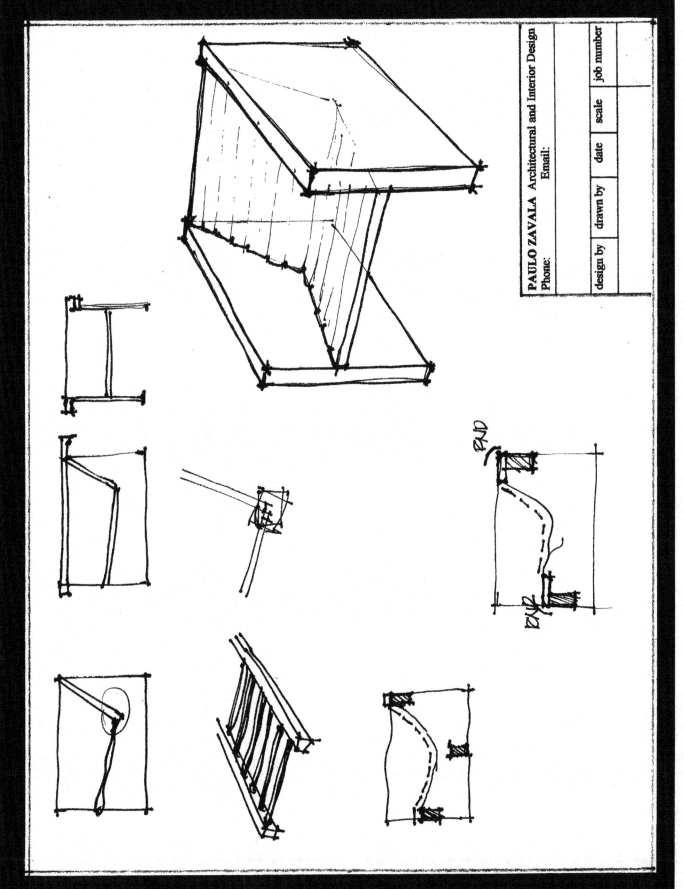

PAULO ZAVALA Architectural and Interior Design
Phone: Email:

design by	drawn by	date	scale	job number

37

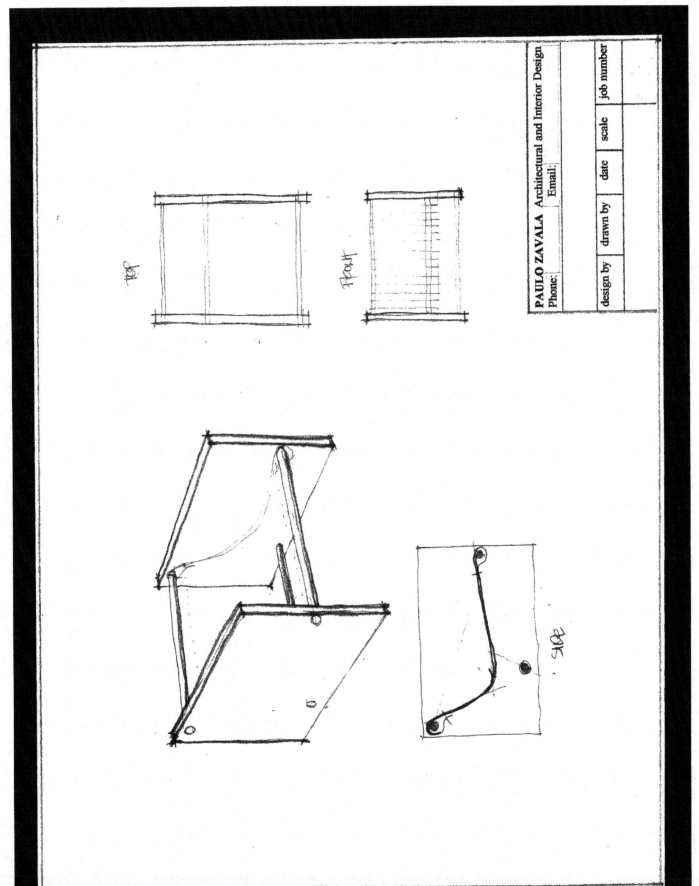

TOP

FRONT

SIDE

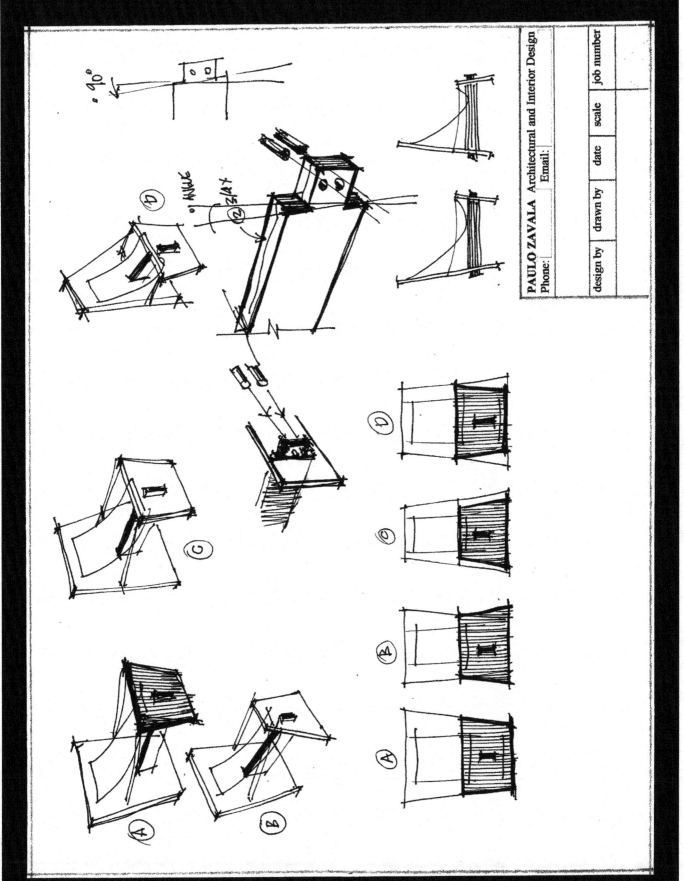

PAULO ZAVALA Architectural and Interior Design
Phone: Email:

design by	drawn by	date	scale	job number

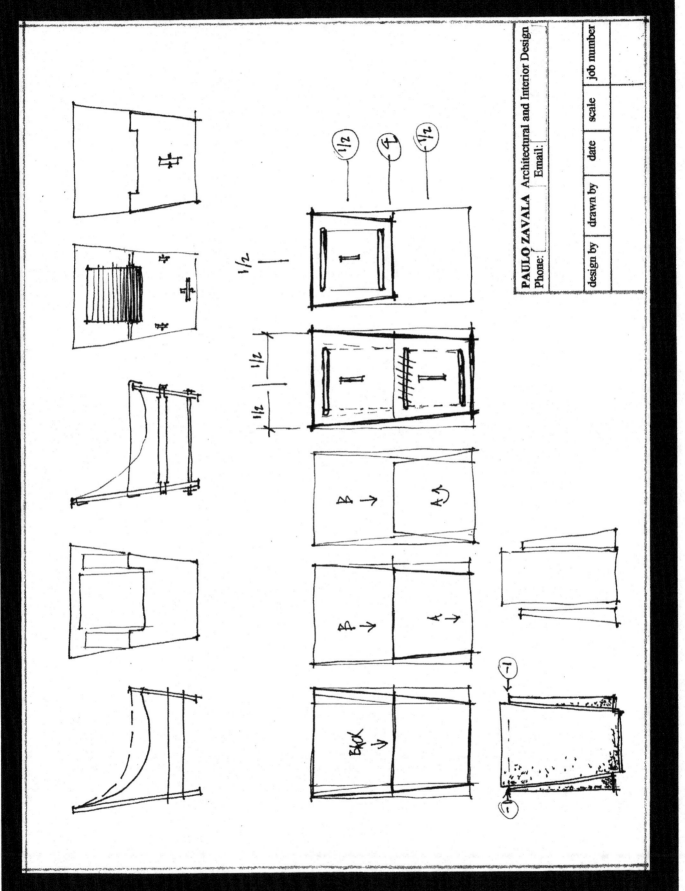

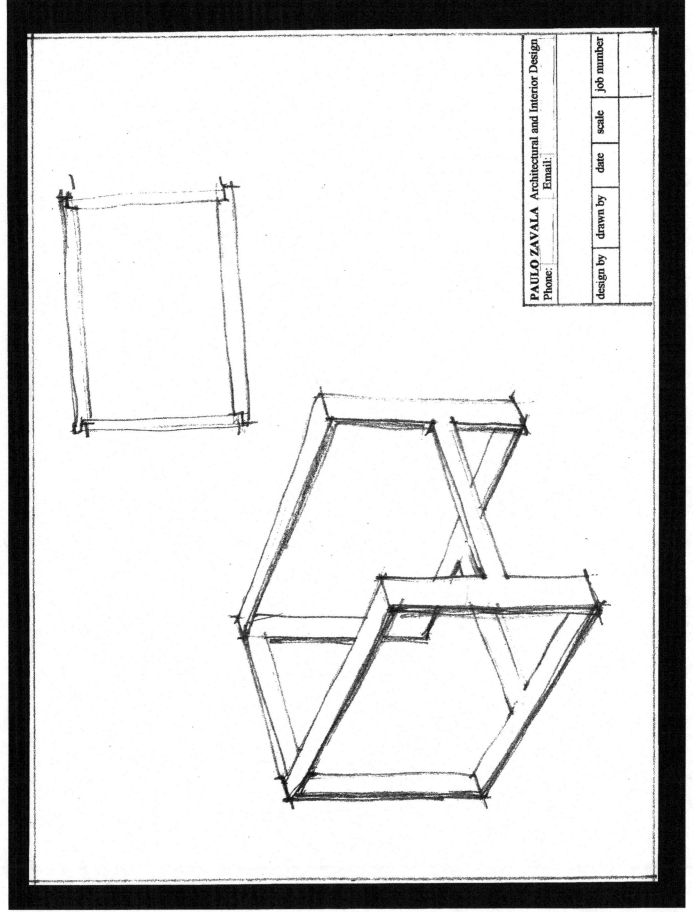

45

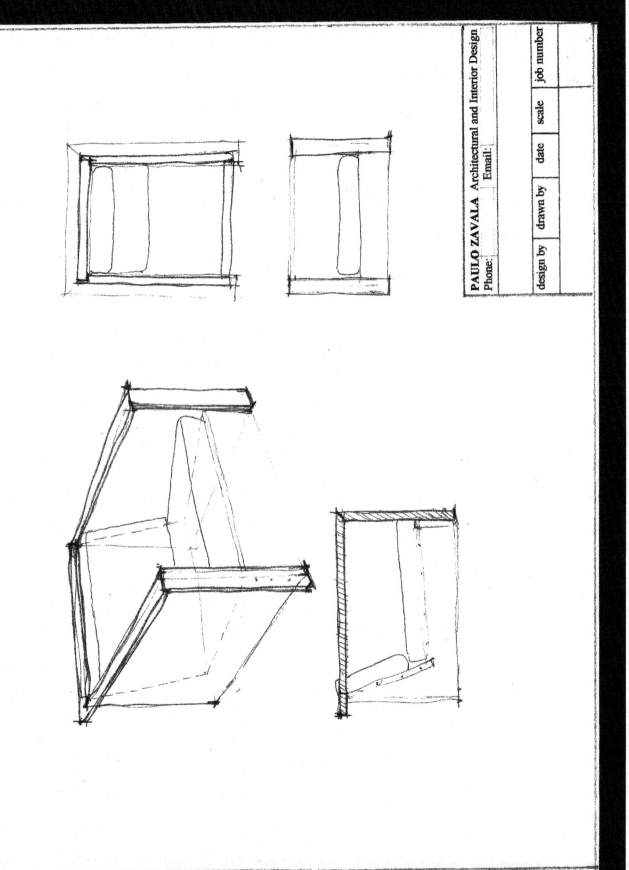

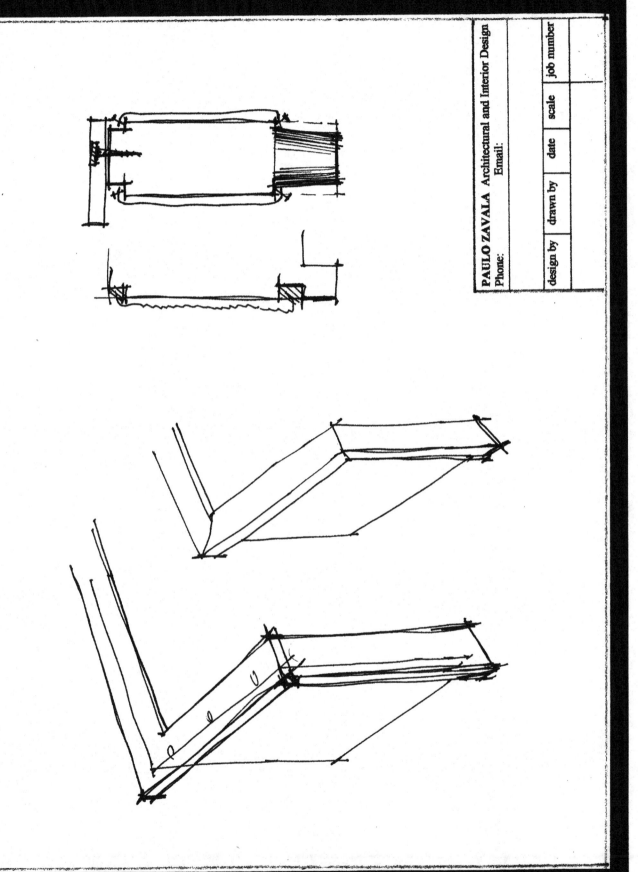

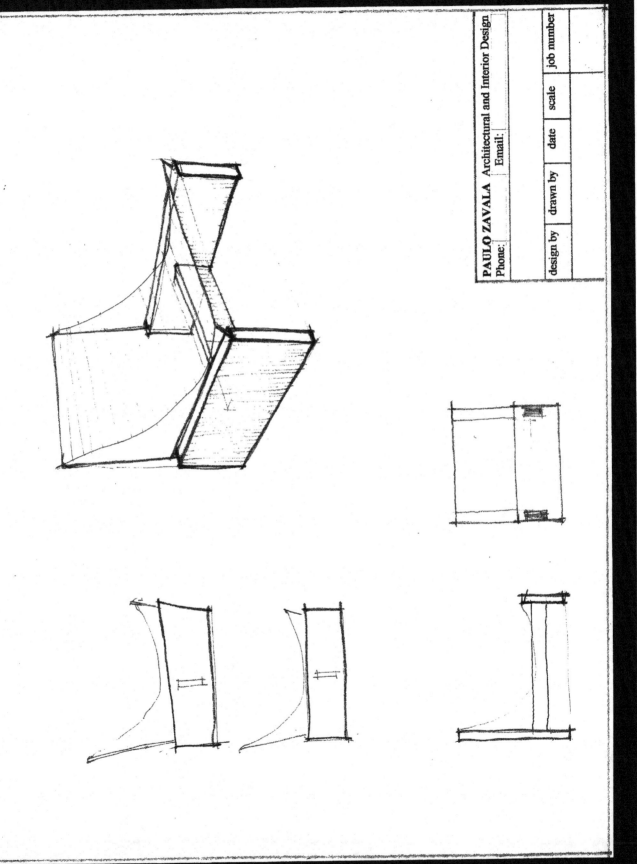

PAULO ZAVALA Architectural and Interior Design
Phone:
Email:

design by	drawn by	date	scale	job number

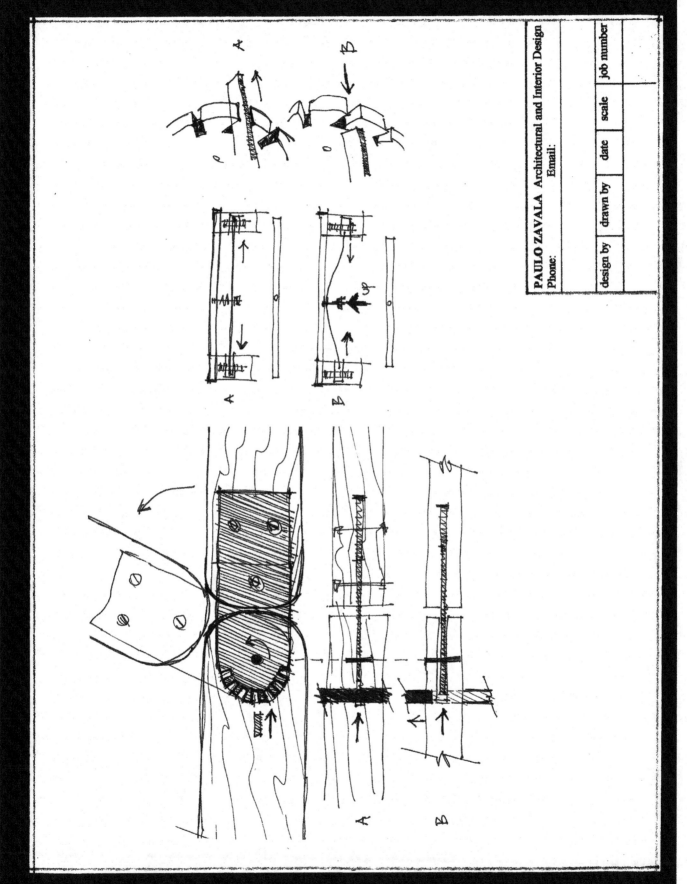

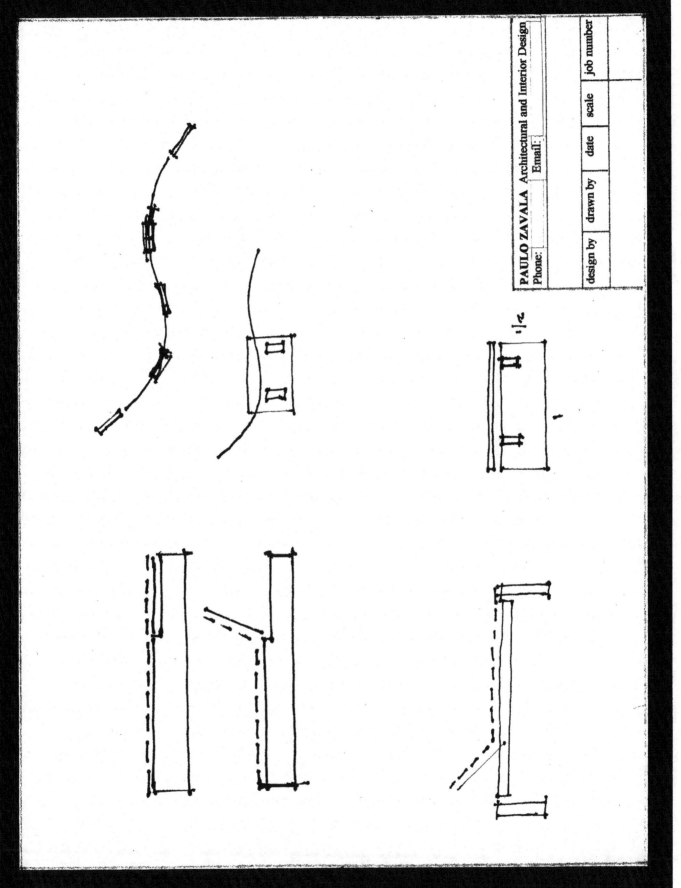

55

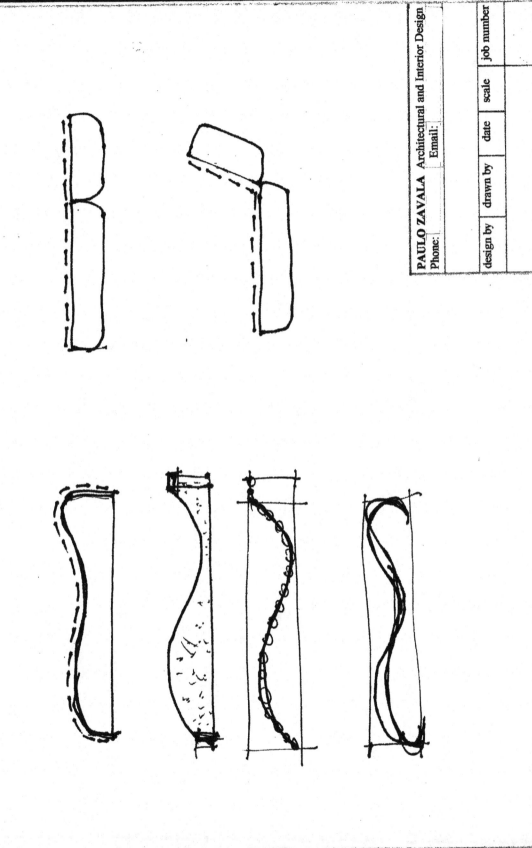

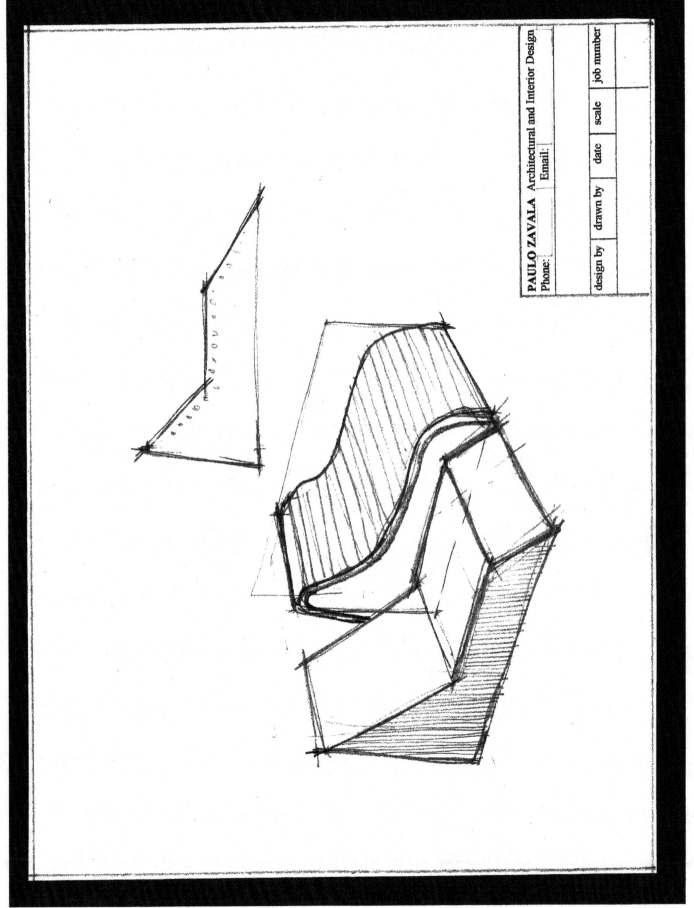

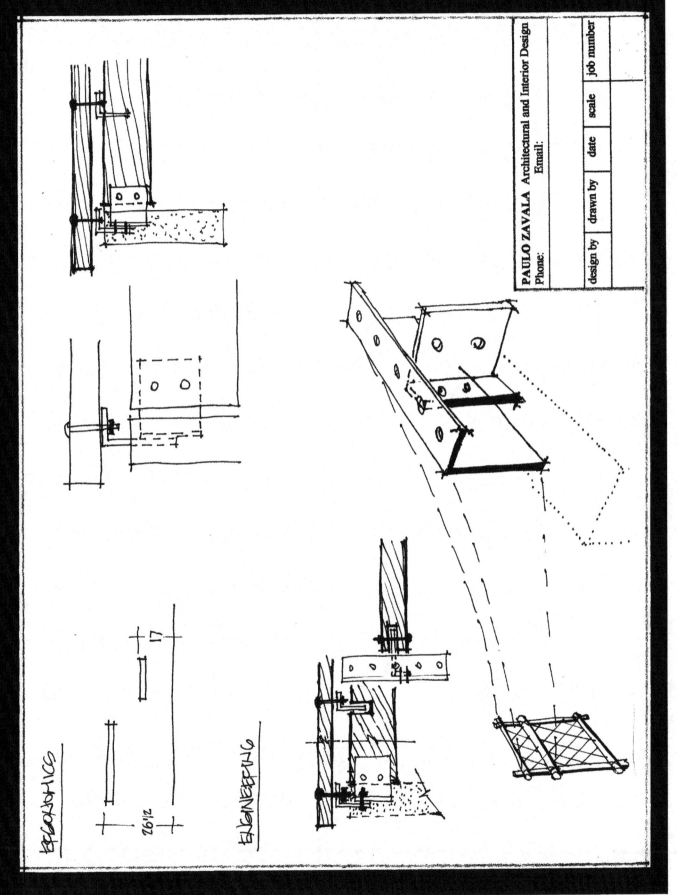

GRAPHICS

ENGINEERING

PAULO ZAVALA Architectural and Interior Design
Phone:
Email:

design by	drawn by	date	scale	job number

61

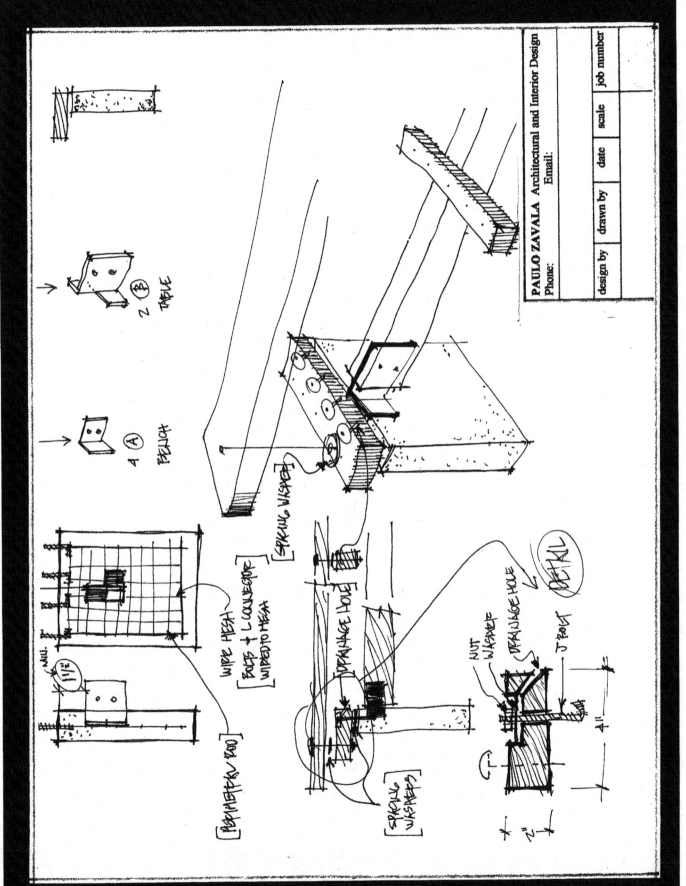

PAULO ZAVALA Architectural and Interior Design
Phone:
Email:

design by	drawn by	date	scale	job number

TABLE

2 (B)

BENCH

4 (A)

SPRING WASHER

WIPE MESH
BOLT & L CONNECTOR
WIPED TO MESH

[ASPHALTEN ROD]

1½"

DRAINAGE HOLE

[SPRING WASHERS]

NUT
WASHER

DRAINAGE HOLE

J BOLT

4"

2"

DETAIL

63

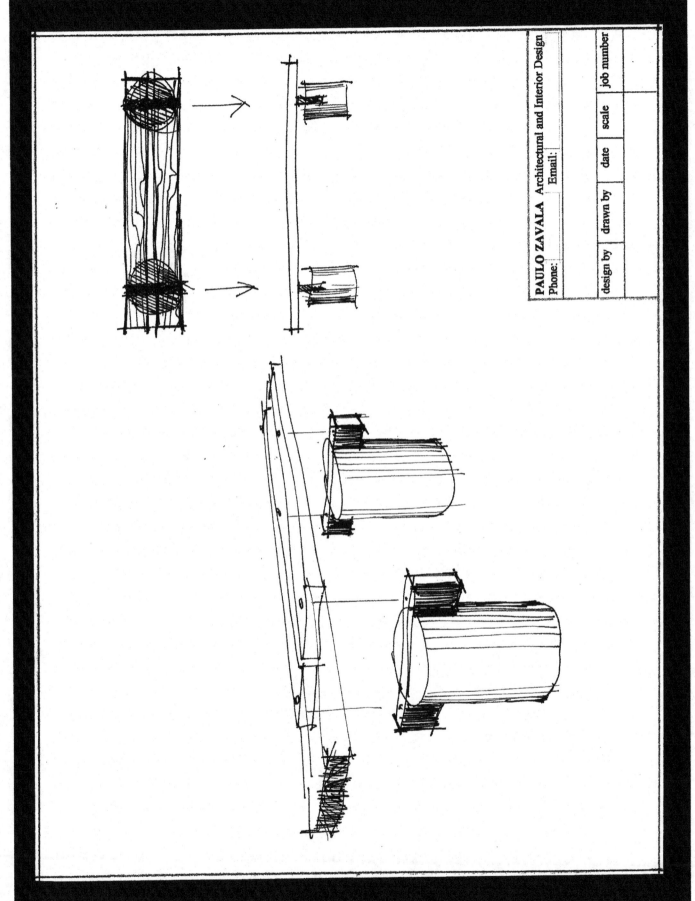

PAULO ZAVALA Architectural and Interior Design
Phone:
Email:

design by	drawn by	date	scale	job number

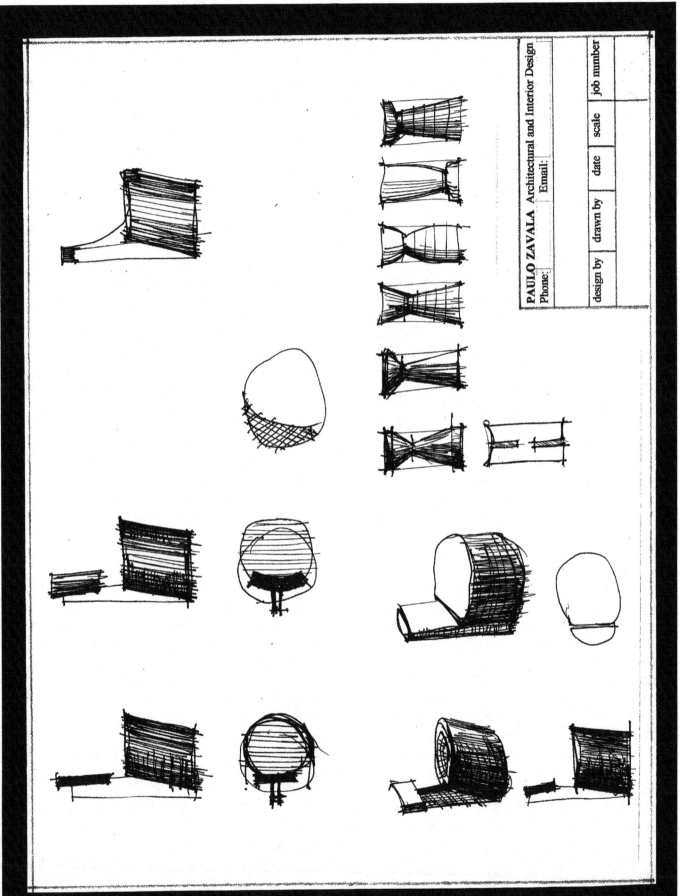

67

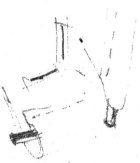

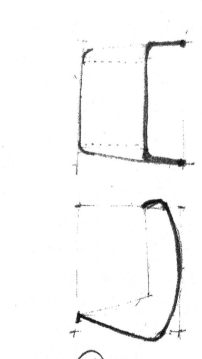

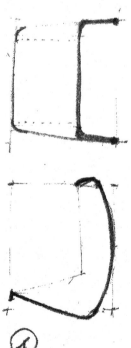

PAULO ZAVALA Architectural and Interior Design
Phone: Email:

design by	drawn by	date	scale	job number

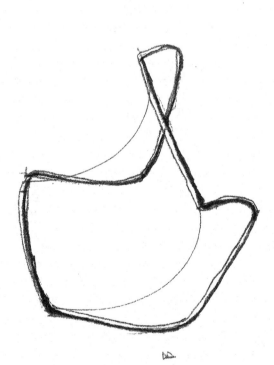

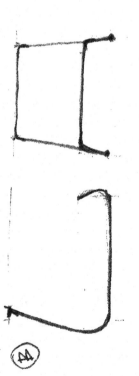

PAULO ZAVALA Architectural and Interior Design
Phone:
Email:

design by	drawn by	date	scale	job number

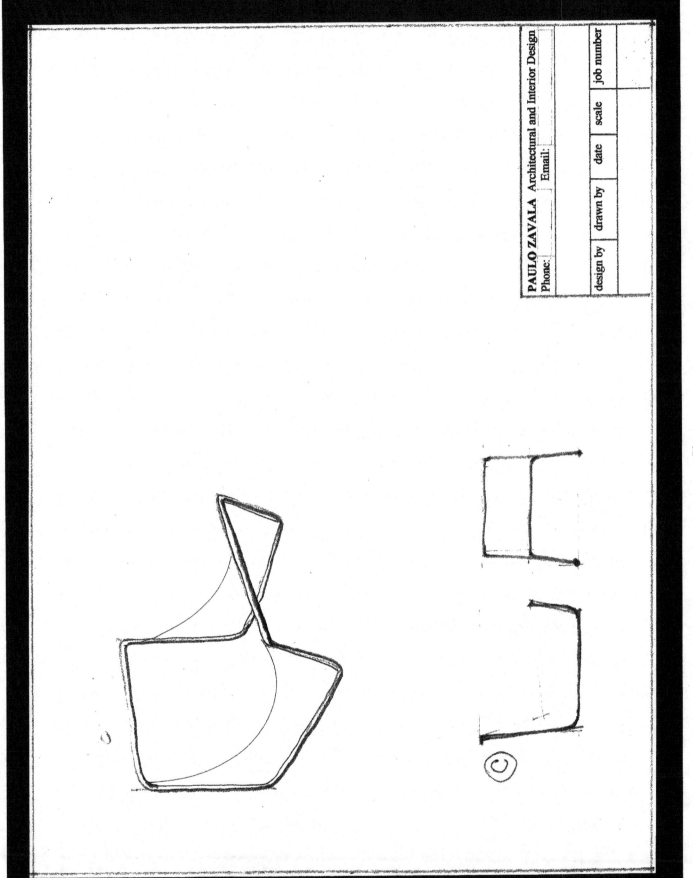

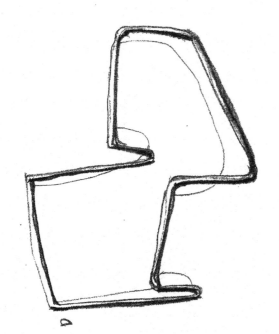

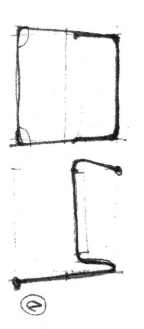

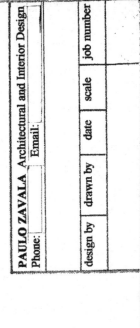

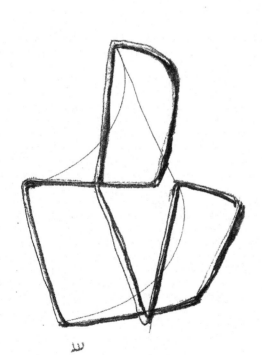

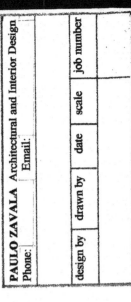

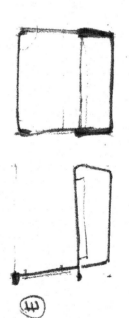

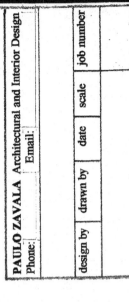

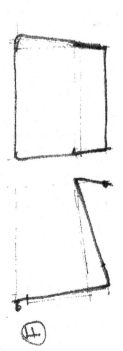

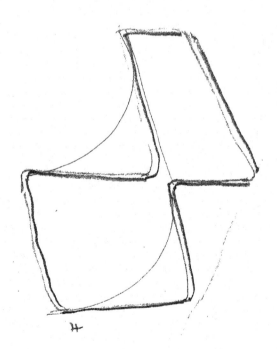

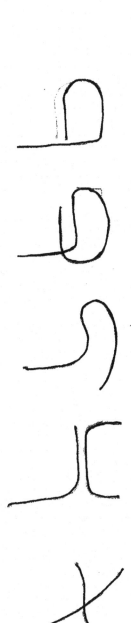

PAULO ZAVALA Architectural and Interior Design
Phone:
Email:

design by	drawn by	date	scale	job number

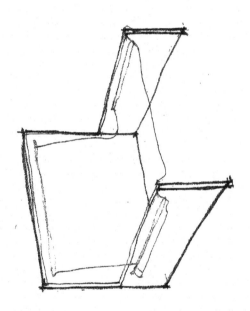

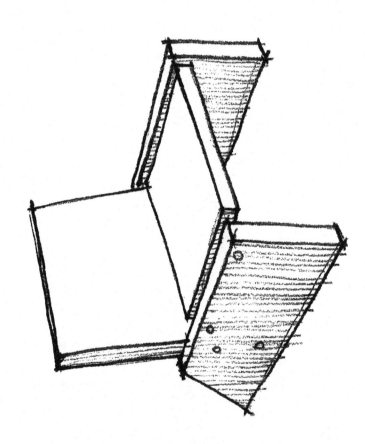

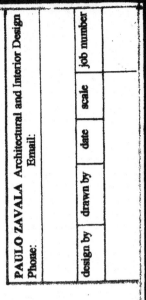

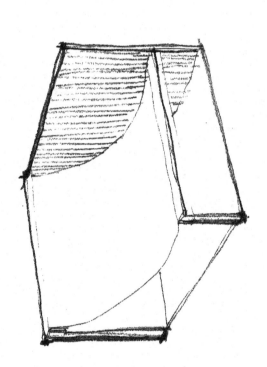

PAULO ZAVALA Architectural and Interior Design
Phone: Email:

design by	drawn by	date	scale	job number

87

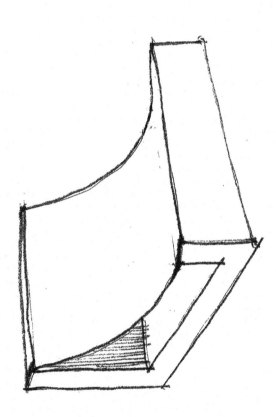

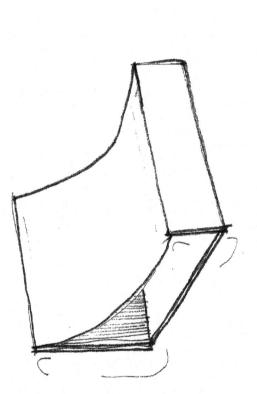

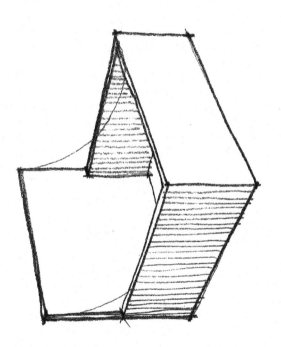

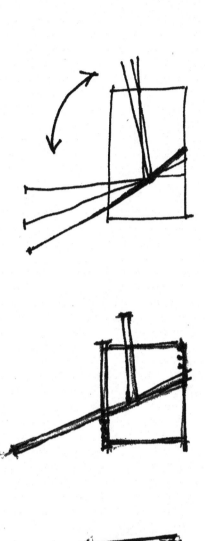

PAULO ZAVALA Architectural and Interior Design
Phone:
Email:

design by	drawn by	date	scale	job number

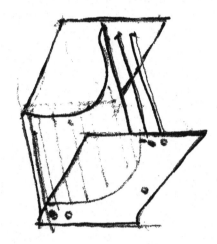

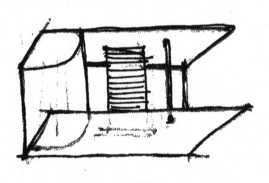

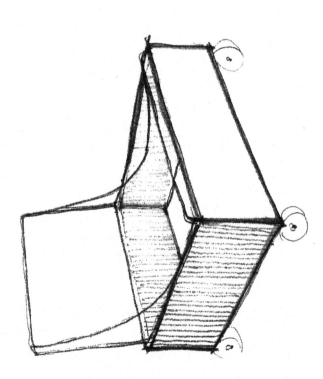

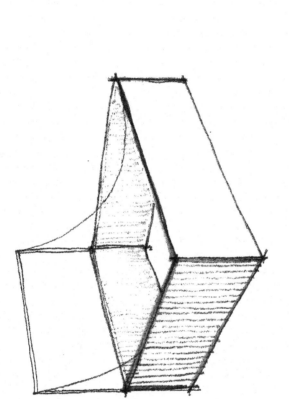

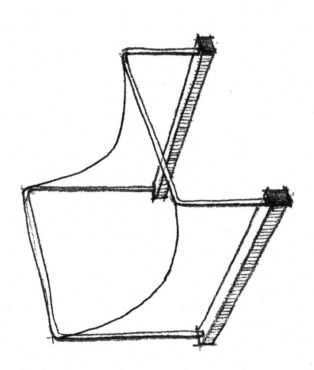

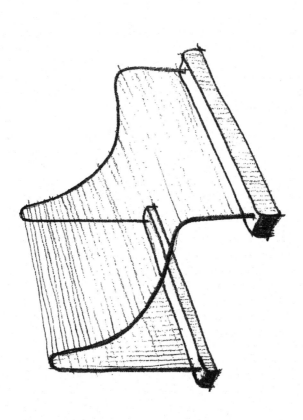

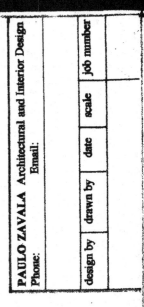

105

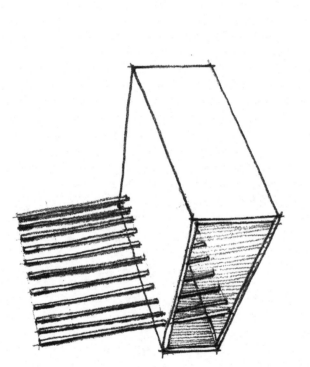

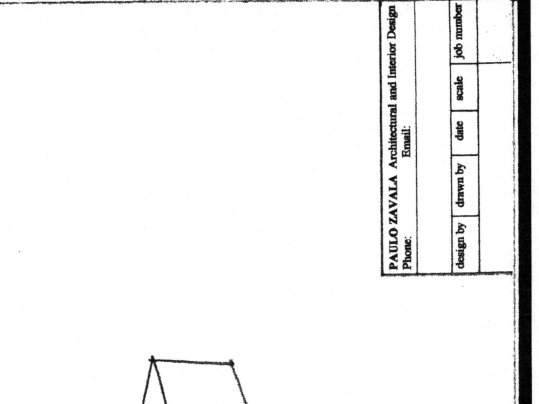

PAULO ZAVALA Architectural and Interior Design
Phone:
Email:

design by	drawn by	date	scale	job number

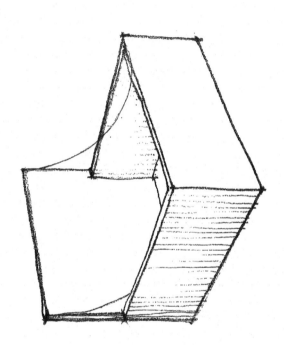

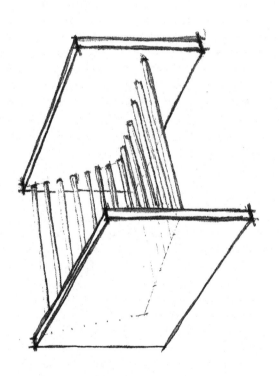

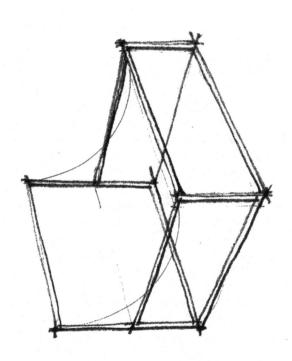

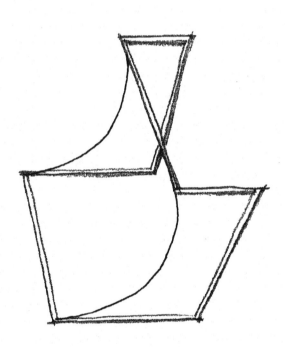

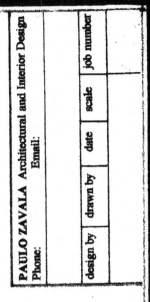
117

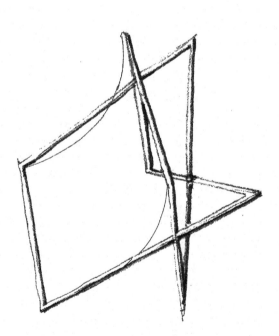

design by	drawn by	date	scale	job number

design by	drawn by	date	scale	job number

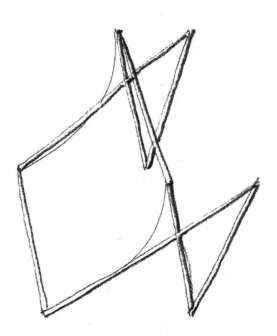

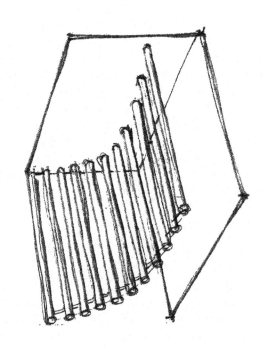

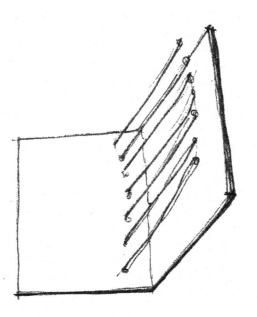

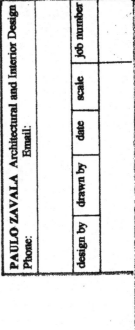

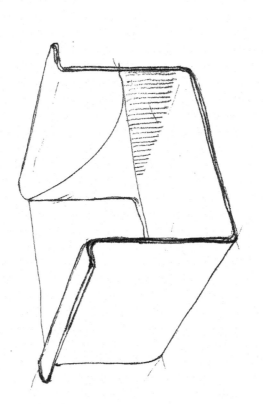

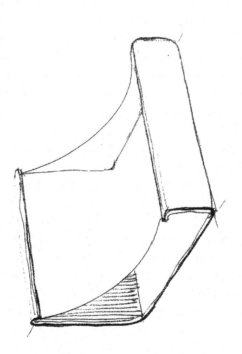

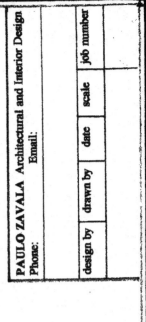

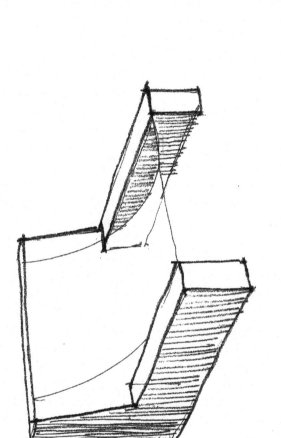

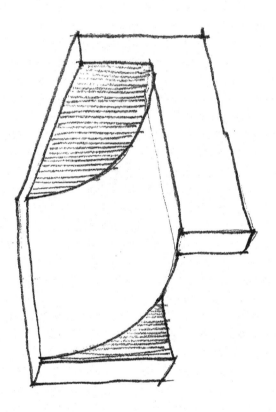

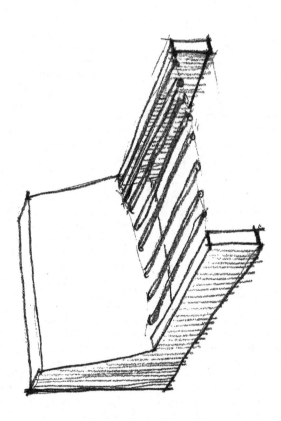

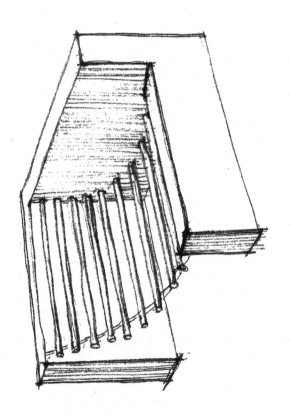

PAULO ZAVALA Architectural and Interior Design
Phone: Email:

design by	drawn by	date	scale	job number